Restaurant Marketing Made Easy

Tools to successfully advertise your local business to a digitally savvy audience

KENNY CHUNG

To Mom and Dad,
whose unwavering support made this book possible.

And in memory of all my favorite restaurants that went out of business far too soon due to the harsh realities of New York City real estate, and general bad taste on the part of everyone who did not support you.

If I had a time machine, I would send this book to you all.

CONTENTS

INTRO:
SO YOU'RE STARTING A
BUSINESS...

Congratulations! Starting any business venture requires a ton of hard work and sacrifice. But the benefits abound: you'll be able to create something of your own design; you'll employ others and give back to the community; and you may even make some money! There are a lot of aspects that you'll have no influence over (like inflation and real estate costs), so it's important that you take advantage of the things that you *can* control.

Marketing is one of the best investments you'll ever make as a business owner. Many of the tactics outlined in this book will require zero overhead, other than the initial time commitment (and however much I've decided to charge for this book).

I have to admit, however, that not all strategies will be easy. But titling this book "Restaurant Marketing Made Easier If You Know All The Right Steps and Sometimes Pay Professionals To Handle The More Difficult Parts" wouldn't have been nearly as catchy. As with anything in life, you have to put in work to see results. The fact that you're reading this right now is a good first step.

In this book, I'll be mostly referring to restaurants and bars, but most of these guidelines are applicable to any small business with a local presence - that includes gift stores, hobby shops, museums, clothing outlets, and probably anything else you can think of.

And finally, I'll be mentioning many online services as examples. Unless otherwise noted, these are for illustrative purposes and are not tacit endorsements. They are intended as a starting point for research and discovery on your part. Where applicable, I will include links to this book's accompanying website (restsite.com) where I'll maintain a list of my personal preferred vendors and partners.

What this book *isn't*

There are countless business texts and resources available to show you how to successfully reduce costs and maximize profits; this is not one of those books. I won't be doling out tips based on behavioral economics studies (like how omitting dollar signs from your menu encourages people to spend more, or that turning up the music increases bar sales). Those items are well-known and outside the purview of this book. I will also not be getting into the legal aspects of starting a business because that knowledge is far outside my wheelhouse (and I'd be doing more damage than good). And while I've previously worked in the food service industry, I cannot help with your supply chain or inventory management issues.

What this book *is*

Instead, this book will focus on best practices and specific marketing tactics that you can start employing today. Each section will have actionable takeaways gleaned from my 10+ years of digital marketing consulting and experience in the local business scene.

As a native New Yorker, I have watched countless restaurants and bars come and go (some of them were personal favorites). I've watched some businesses adapt to the internet and flourish with new avenues of reaching customers, while others fell behind and had to shutter their doors. I believe that everybody benefits when local businesses thrive, and this book is an attempt on my part to help where I can.

What we'll cover

This book does not need to be read sequentially (feel free to skip around and find what's most relevant to your situation). That said, it is organized into five parts:

- **Part I. Your web presence.**
We'll cover: how to prioritize your online efforts as well as best practices for maintaining your website/social media profiles; tips on food photography; and the types of content customers are expecting when they search for you.

- **Part II. Marketing your business.**
We'll look at how you can increase awareness of your business and gain new customers via search marketing, hosting events, leveraging social media platforms (*e.g.* Instagram), and more.

- **Part III. Keep customers coming back.**
These are tried-and-true customer retention strategies that will foster repeat business.

- **Part IV. If things turn sour...**
We'll look at the worst case scenario and what you can do if your business suffers an insurmountable obstacle (or several), and what your next steps should be.

- **Part V. Interviews with the experts.**
Lastly, I have interviewed some of my favorite restaurant owners and subject matter experts; you'll find snippets of these conversations sprinkled throughout certain sections with full transcripts at the end of the book.

For the sake of convenience, I have also made many resources available for free at restsite.com

PART I:
YOUR WEB
PRESENCE

1.
WHY GO DIGITAL?

Establishing a web presence is one of the simplest things you can do to help your business succeed. However, simple doesn't always mean easy. It doesn't begin and end with just having a website; you need to have a *good* website. It also means making sure that your information across the web is accurate. And that you're listening to what people are saying about you and responding accordingly.

Among the chief benefits of actively maintaining your online presence:

- **Controlling the messaging.** If you're not the one informing people about your business, then other websites will (and not always accurately or in a positive light). Ensure the right message and tone is conveyed throughout all consumer touchpoints.

- **Business updates.** Keep customers and potential patrons updated on your goings-on, and foster excitement for upcoming news/events.

- **Online reputation management.** Monitor your mentions for bad reviews or false information, and prevent more of the same.

- **Expanding your customer base.** Build a cohort of (loyal and future) customers for marketing purposes.

- **Creating foot traffic.** Lastly but most importantly, convert online tire-kickers into in-person sales.

Controlling the messaging

People go online primarily for information. For businesses, reliable sources include search engines like Google, business aggregators like Yelp, and articles from local food critics. These sources will often try to infer things about your business. For instance, is that particular dish vegan or vegetarian? Are your recipes Indian or Pakistani in origin? Do you close earlier on weekends? How much would that smoked rib sandwich cost with onion rings instead of fries?

As a business owner, it behooves you to be the source of truth. If not, then inaccuracies will spread, which are hard to completely rectify. Practically speaking, this means you should publish helpful information that conveys your brand messaging (what your product is, who you are, what your philosophy is, etc.). Another way to think about it: if a journalist or blogger wanted to write an article covering your restaurant opening, what information would they need? And are you providing said information on your website or other online platforms in an easy-to-find, concise manner?

Business updates

Businesses never remain static. Menus change. Prices change. Sometimes, even whole cuisines and business models change. As a customer, there's nothing more deflating or disappointing than being misled. If your outdated website menu lists a dish at $22, but it's since increased to $30, customers may feel deceived once they sit down and peruse the menu. If you've been unable to restock a rare/specialty ingredient for weeks, customers who make the trip specifically for that dish will be frustrated. If you're throwing a special ticketed event, but you're solely relying on posters on the wall of your restaurant to get the word out, then turnout will likely underwhelm.

It can be difficult to find time to make all of these changes yourself, but there are other methods of communicating with your customer base that will be covered in the marketing section in Part II.

Online reputation management

Nothing can sink a business faster than a bad review (or many). Regardless of how you feel about the (professional and amateur) food critic space - if you don't pay attention to how others are talking about you, then you're setting yourself up for failure. Reacting to and changing your practices based on customer feedback will lead to better reviews in the future, as well as repeat business. For instance, multiple reviewers may mention that your menu offers nothing for pescatarians or those with a gluten intolerance; or that your beer selection is too limited; or that there's no changing table in the bathrooms. Those are easy-to-address complaints. And if those pain points originate from online review sites like Yelp, you can reply publicly and show future readers that you're a responsive business owner who addresses customer concerns. Conversely, if there's a specific reason why you can't accommodate all customers, it provides a platform to explain your reasoning (and hopefully, future readers will be empathetic).

Expanding your customer base

The best way to discover and reach potential customers is online. Sure, you set up a clipboard at your host station and take down names, phone numbers, and email addresses, but very few people will have the time or inclination to fill those out; and you'll only be limited to the people who are already in your establishment. On the internet, all you need is an email address or a Facebook Like to start marketing to individuals en masse.

Creating foot traffic

Most importantly, a carefully maintained web presence will bring people into your physical space. Your website will showcase all the things you offer, with beautiful high quality photos and inviting descriptions. You've maintained accurate listings across multiple online business directories, and people use them to discover that you've recently made exciting menu changes. You provide multiple avenues for booking a reservation, reducing the friction of getting people through the door.

2.
MEET CUSTOMERS WHERE THEY ARE

One of the basic tenets of successful marketing is to serve the right message at the right time via the right channel; in other words, meet customers where they are. People's online behaviors can be generalized pretty well: they go to restaurant websites to look at menus; they use Yelp for reviews and customer photos; they navigate to Google Maps for directions.

New businesses may not always have the hours available to manage a website/multiple social media accounts, or the financial resources to hire someone to handle these tasks. Therefore, it's important to be selective about where you actively update your information.

While not a wholly comprehensive list, here are a few examples of how and where you should engage your online customers:

- **Menu updates:** your website, Instagram, Facebook, food ordering platforms

- **Glamour shots:** website, Instagram, Facebook, Yelp

- **Your location if you're a mobile business:** Twitter, Facebook, Instagram

- **Special holiday hours:** Google, Yelp, Facebook, Instagram

- **Responding to customer messages:** Yelp, Facebook, Twitter

- **Special promotions:** email, Yelp, Facebook, Instagram, Twitter

- **Current inventory:** Instagram, Facebook, Twitter

- **Events:** email, Yelp, Facebook, Instagram

Of course, you may find that your business only cultivates a following on one specific social network. If that's the case, then you're in luck since your workload will be significantly decreased. However, you should still create profiles on all these services; if you don't plan on maintaining them, you can explicitly direct people to the platform where you're most likely to provide regular updates.

3.
DOMAIN NAMES AND SOCIAL MEDIA HANDLES

Be sure to do some research on how you'll refer to your business online. Perform a quick Google search to make sure that your name won't be negatively misconstrued (and that Google will not automatically correct it to a completely unrelated phrase). Also make sure that you can buy the domain name and that all other social media handles are available. While not 100% necessary, using the same handle across all social media platforms will make things easier for your audience to remember.

4.
BEST PRACTICES FOR MANAGING YOUR WEBSITE

Now it's time to set up your website. For a lot of customers, it will be the front door to your business, so it's pivotal that you make a good first impression.

Website vs mobile app

If anyone ever offers to create a mobile app for your small business, feel free to ignore their message. Apps are only useful if you have multiple locations like a chain/franchise and have a robust ordering system in place. For most local restaurants, this is too much infrastructure to manage. More often than not, it's a ploy to keep charging your business money every time you need to make small updates to the app, which will happen anytime you want to change your menu, or if a new smartphone becomes popular and it has different display requirements that your app wasn't futureproofed against (perhaps by design).

A website is a far more elegant solution. Most people can create a website themselves (using Wordpress, Squarespace, or some other user-friendly interface), or they can hire someone to design and code it. And as long as you make sure that the web designers explain how you can update pages yourself after their contracted work is over, it should be relatively simple to maintain.

One last consideration is to make sure your website is mobile-friendly. In other words, when the website is sized down, all the text is legible, and any buttons are big enough for a finger to tap on accurately. Search engines like Google even penalize websites that are not mobile-friendly. If you have any doubts, sign up for Google Search Console, which is a free service that will let you know if there are any issues with your site (See the Analytics and Tracking section in chapter 4 for more information). Per Google's guidelines, you should ideally have a single website that scales properly based on the user's device. Long gone are the days where separate mobile versions of the website (such as m.business.com) are necessary (or recommended).

Website accuracy

Accuracy is the key to trust. Nobody wants customers to be disappointed if an online menu was inaccurate, or worse yet, if store hours were wrong and the customer can't even sit down for a meal after making the trip.

While your website doesn't need to be updated every day to reflect daily specials, certain items are expected to be accurate at all times. This includes standard hours of operation and any special policies. If you're having holiday hours or are closed for a private event, you should list this information somewhere on your site (depending on your website template, an announcement bar at the top of your site is a common solution, though you can also include it as a simple text paragraph on your homepage). Other features that may require more frequent updates (*e.g.* daily specials or rotating beer taps) should be handled on other platforms that are more conducive to passive marketing, such as Instagram or Facebook. In all cases, your website should make a point to mention where to find the latest information (if it's not the site itself).

Online menus

Menus are the lifeblood of any restaurant, so it's no surprise that users expect restaurant websites to have them readily available. The most common method to help users find them is to include a link in your main site navigation. From there, you can also link to your individual menus (brunch, lunch, dinner, happy hour, late night, beer, wine, etc.) if applicable.

Note that it's a common practice for most website templates to label their main navigation as "MENU." However, doing so on a restaurant site can lead to confusion. For this, I can propose two solutions - either don't collapse the menu at all (*i.e.* show all navigation items at all times), or simply use a hamburger icon (parallel horizontal lines) to depict the menu toggle; this has become a widely understood symbol for both mobile and desktop users.

The format of your menus is also worth considering. Many businesses rely on PDFs, which have both benefits and disadvantages. On the plus side, you can upload the same file that's used to print your physical menus, eliminating the need to duplicate work. Secondly, if you make wholesale changes to your menu, you can just replace the entire PDF instead of editing individual items.

However, PDFs present certain challenges. They can become a pain to manage, depending on your online content management system (CMS). A common problem is that it may become possible for people to find outdated versions of your menu via search engines, or if the files are directly linked from other websites. Lastly, depending on a user's computer or devices settings, they may end up inadvertently downloading the PDF instead of viewing it in their browser, which is a poor user experience.

The best approach to address these issues is to have a text-based menu on a webpage. This does require more maintenance if you're making minor (or major) changes to your offerings. I would recommend this method if your menu doesn't change more than once a quarter. I would absolutely not recommend creating HTML menus for things that rotate often, like beer or wine lists. There are services whose main functionality is to allow you to keep such minutiae up-to-date (such as BeerMenus). Text-based menus are also easier for search engines and other services to parse/display on their own platforms, which will increase your exposure. However, one major disadvantage of an HTML menu is that it will be harder to keep the style consistent with the on-brand print version used in your restaurant.

Perhaps the compromise that works best for most businesses is to install a PDF viewer plugin that combines the best of both worlds. With this solution, you can upload a PDF version of your menu, and then embed it on the HTML page. This makes things easier to manage, and there's no risk of users going offsite or downloading the PDF accidentally.

In all cases, you should date your menus. While nobody plans for it, there may be a chance that your website maintenance efforts lapse. If your menu is three years old, the customer should be aware of this fact and plan accordingly.

Reservations

Ironically, now that everyone has a phone in their pocket, more people avoid speaking on the phone if alternatives are available. Therefore, you should provide multiple methods for people to make a reservation. The most common method is a service like OpenTable, which handles this process through their platform (also available as a plug-in for your site and via their app).

If you have a private space that can accommodate larger groups for events, you should have a dedicated page on your site that explicitly mentions these amenities. On this page, highlight the capacity of the space and what types of services you provide (catering, drink specials, etc.). It's not necessary to list prices here, as it may inform your competitors or prematurely drive some users away. Instead, you should include an email address or a form that users can fill out (an email address may be slightly better, as your reply is less likely to be filtered to spam when you respond). I would highly recommend setting up a shared email address specifically for bookings, which will keep communications organized.

Last but not least, you should also have your restaurant's phone number listed on every page of your site (usually in the header and/or footer). This will allow traditionalists to call and actually speak to a human being to make a reservation.

Delivery

Similar to reservations, you should provide website visitors multiple ways to order delivery if that's an option. Again, a phone number will be invaluable. However, for some businesses, phone calls may not the most efficient method. There may be background noises that cause things to get lost in translation, or there may be menu items that are hard to pronounce/hear. Text-based communication for orders is therefore more foolproof.

Services like Seamless or GrubHub are the most popular. However, you'll have to keep your menu updated, and to make sure any special/holiday hours are maintained. And of course, those commission fees can add up. It may be worth the cost, however, since enrolling in these services provides more exposure to your business, and users will discover your restaurant on the platform in the midst of their hungry browsing. Also, for larger/more complicated meals, having every detail meticulously written out makes orders fulfilment significantly easier. Finally, it's much easier for users to complete orders via credit card on these services compared to doing so over the phone.

Directions

You absolutely must include the address of your business on your website, preferably on every page (typically in the footer, and prominently displayed on the homepage). Additionally, if your business is hard to find, then you should have a dedicated directions page. For instance, if you're not close to public transportation; if you're located inside a mall/airport/other complex; or if there are specific parking lot or valet directions that Google or Apple Maps may not take into account.

On this page, you should have detailed instructions, a map of your location, and a link to Google Maps with your location pre-filled. If you're near a landmark or tourist destination, you should also include those as a reference point. Taking these steps should cover all of your bases.

Personnel and other connections

In this modern age, many chefs are becoming more popular than the restaurants for whom they work. If you're lucky enough to employ one of these superstars, you should take advantage of their clout by creating an "about" page dedicated to them on your website. This will be an additional entry point for web users who are specifically searching for them.

Even if your head chef isn't well-known, it makes sense to create a page about them as a sort of credentials list. You should include other places where they've worked, as an indirect way of conveying the quality of your food and service. Many people also place a high value on supporting minority- or female-owned businesses, so this is also an opportunity to showcase your personnel accordingly.

Lastly, you may be part of larger restaurant group. In many of these cases, the parent company will control the look and feel of all sites to be more standardized. However, if you're the webmaster of the parent company or have complete control of a child site, it's in your best interest to create links between the related restaurants. From the main hospitality group website, this allows users to see all available restaurants and browse them individually. This also lends credibility to newly opened restaurants. Additionally, if possible, every child restaurant site should include links to all of its siblings. Oftentimes this is done via links in the footer, with a lead-in such as "visit our other restaurants." An additional benefit is that search engines will use these links to discover new businesses, and the links will lend some authority.

Analytics and tracking

When business is booming, you probably won't pay too much attention to your website users. But what if you need an extra boost? That's when analytics and tracking become a valuable ally. There are a lot of free analytics services that can help you figure out how people use your site (Google Analytics is the industry standard). All you have to do is include a short code snippet on every page, and the platform will let you know how users interact with your content. And if you implement more advanced click tracking, you can even figure out when people perform any action, like clicking onto an external link (like a PDF menu or OpenTable/Seamless).

Additionally, you should append tracking tags to all of your marketing campaigns (*e.g.* paid search, banner ads, or social media). This will allow you to segment your website audience appropriately in order to compare and contrast which channels are working the best.

What do you do with all this data? At the most base level, you should determine which parts of your website aren't working as intended. Are people not clicking onto the page that lists your menus? Then maybe you should make those links more prominent (or rename them). Are paid Instagram users not doing anything once they reach your site? Maybe you should reallocate your spend to other channels. Are people reaching your "about us" page and immediately leaving after 3 seconds? Maybe you should enhance the content.

A/B testing is the easiest way to make reversible changes and test their efficacy, and there are also many vendors out there that can help you implement this in a safe and timely manner.

Email newsletter signup

If you plan on starting an email newsletter, then you need a method of collecting contact information. Typically, websites will include a popup interstitial on the homepage, or a dedicated text field in the header or footer. Be sure to include a general idea of what you'll be sending people. See the Email Newsletters section in Chapter 12 for more best practices.

News, events, and blogs

Search engine crawlers and users will routinely return to your website if you're making regular updates. Here are some intuitive content formats that you can leverage:

• **News section.** This is where you can post updates about your business, like seasonal menu items, new hours, awards, notable new hires, participation in local festivals, etc.

• **Events calendar.** If you're regularly hosting events open to the public, you should maintain an events calendar. The best calendar is one where each event has its own dedicated page, which will allow people to easily share specific events.

• **Blogs.** For all other in-depth content, a dedicated blog is the best way to display goings-on relevant to your business. This could include items like recipes from your chefs, stories about how your employees are giving back to the community, recognition in the space, or other local and social news.

Everything else

This section was by no means a fully comprehensive list. Each customer is different in their wants and needs. Some people may want to know what your payment options are (there's a big divide now between cash-only and cash-free establishments). Other consistently growing audience segments are pet owners and parents. If your business is dog friendly, you should mention that up front as not many restaurants and bars fit that bill. And if you're a bar that's kid-friendly, you should mention that for the same reasons.

5.
PHOTOGRAPHY

Like the saying goes, you eat with your eyes first. Commissioning professional, high quality photos of your business and food will likely be one of the best investments you'll make. Not only will you be able to feature the photos on your website, but you can also repurpose them for social media, online directories like Yelp, and on delivery services like Seamless/GrubHub.

However, if you don't have the budget for a professional photographer, here are some general tips for taking great photos:

1. Lighting is 90% of what makes a good photo.

Good lighting, specifically. While dim lighting is great for ambience, it doesn't lend itself to great or inviting business photos. In darker environments, the camera has to work harder to capture details and the photographer has to work harder to keep things in focus.

While subject lighting is a full book's worth of instruction unto itself, a good rule of thumb is to use indirect lighting. Take photos during the daytime if possible - near a window where the sun not shining directly at your subject. This also means that if you're using a camera flash unit, avoid pointing it directly at what you're shooting. You can use a diffuser or a light umbrella (or simply point the flash unit in a different direction). This should prevent your photos from looking harsh or washed out.

If you're using a DSLR or prosumer camera with manual functions, don't set the aperture too wide because the result could lead to only parts of the dish being in focus (this takes a good eye to get right, otherwise it looks cheap and gimmicky). Shutter speed should not be too much a factor with good lighting and a static subject (the only exceptions might be smoke rising off the dish, or bubbles in a drink, but those are fringe cases). Lastly, dial down the ISO because food photos shouldn't look grainy (again, good lighting will help). Most of the time, the auto (or green) function on the camera should serve your purposes as long as you pre-focus. If you want to get fancy, then I recommend using the aperture-priority mode with a depth of field that keeps the entire dish in focus but blurs any background elements.

If all else fails, most modern smartphones have great cameras that can automatically adjust for lighting and have reliable point focusing. However, note that most camera phone flashes are objectively terrible. While not ideal, in a pinch, you can use a two-phone setup - one with the flashlight as lighting (using a piece of paper to diffuse/bounce the light, and the other one to snap the shot; for the most consistent results, this will probably require two or more people and a ton of trial and error.

2. Take photos of your most popular dishes.

This should be a given. If someone Googles a dish you're known for, they should be able to easily find an image of it. This gives them an idea of how much food to expect, and will also help them decide whether or not to order it. In the internet and social media age, people most definitely research and plan meals beforehand, so you should take advantage of this behavior. When you post photos on your website (or on Yelp), include descriptive captions. Also name your image files appropriately; this will help search engines find the images and provide them to users specifically looking for them. See the Organic Search section in Chapter 8 for more specific best practices.

3. Take photos of your space, including the store front.

Diners like to feel comfortable with their restaurant decisions before sitting down, and even before making a reservation. Photos of the space can convey a lot of information that text cannot. They can show people how casual or intimate a meal will be. They can help customers spot where the entrance is when they're driving or walking down the street (this is especially important if the restaurant is located inside a hotel or food hall, for instance). At a glance, they can help people book a venue for a party/event if you adequately showcase your private space. And they can highlight specialty features, like an outdoor space, TVs showing sports games, a comprehensive whiskey/beer/wine list, or even fun activities like bar games (darts, arcades, board games, etc.).

4. Feature customers in photos.

Nothing makes people want to join in on the fun like seeing other people having a good time. Photos of smiling customers enjoying their meal and a round of drinks will go a long way to humanize your space. From photos, potential customers can also learn about the dress code, and can see if the typical clientele is hip young millennials, stuffy older business types in three-piece suits, or somewhere in between. Of course, most people do not want to be bothered during their meal for a posed photo. To this, I offer two solutions - a soft opening/customer appreciation event, or leveraging photos taken by others. Each of these options require a more detailed deep dive (learn more about special events in the Hosting Events section in Chapter 13, and more about leveraging photo assets in the Photography section Chapter 5). Just be sure to include a notice to patrons that there will be photos or filming occurring throughout the event.

* * *

One last note on food photography - only some foods lend themselves to attractive presentation. For example: a brightly colored fresh sashimi platter, a perfectly cooked medium rare steak with a charred exterior; an ice cream cone topped with all the fixins; a bowl of ramen with all the accoutrements carefully arranged on top; a sandwich piled high with more meats than you can count on a lightly toasted sesame baguette.

However, even if you expertly plate some dishes with multiple carefully placed sauce drizzles, some foods are simply not photogenic. Stews and soups, for instance, do not photograph well (especially dark ones). Most curries do not look appetizing in photos. Meatloaf, while delicious, is hard to make visually appealing. A lot of steamed Chinese dishes and dumplings look off-white and lumpy. Even pizza with sauce on top looks bland compared to slices with cheese and/or toppings at the forefront.

This is just reality, and there's only so much you can do. Creative plating, or adding things like a sprig of thyme may seem like a good idea, but be sure that if someone orders that dish, what arrives at their table is a close visual approximation.

There are some tried-and-true tips that can help with "ugly" foods. Displaying a cross-section of a dish that would otherwise look monotone and bland (like a chicken pot pie, beef wellington, etc.) will add some contrast. Taking an overhead photo of the entire table spread will allow you to include some "boring" foods alongside the exciting ones without drawing too much attention to their drabness.

And specifically for simple looking drinks, a common approach is to feature the ingredients that go into that drink. For a beer brewed with citrus fruit, you can place some oranges and limes next to a Teku glass filled with the beer. For a cocktail, you can photograph it next to bottles of its constituent parts and whole garnishes.

Using other people's photos

It can be tempting to repurpose photos that other people have taken at your restaurant and re-upload them to your website or social media. However, be warned that you may not have a legal right to do so. The person who took the photo is typically the copyright holder, and if they upload to a service like Yelp or Seamless, those companies also have a (non-exclusive) right to use them. The proper approach would be to contact the person who took/uploaded the photo, verify that they took it, and ask if you can use it on your website or other digital platforms. Once you have written consent (via email, or in a social media comment, etc.), then you can use it as part of your marketing. Be sure to obtain a high quality version of the file as well.

Another option is to use photos that have been cleared for commercial purposes. You can routinely search for your own business on sites like Flickr, and if the photographer has opted to allow commercial use of their photos, then you're clear to use them on your website. Just be sure to read the fine print of the Creative Commons, as you may need to credit them appropriately.

Video content

Once your photo assets are up to snuff, it may seem like a logical next step to create video content. However, most of the time, the returns will be minimal. Unless you're already shooting a professional commercial, creating high quality videos for online consumption is a very expensive and time-consuming process.

Instead, you should rely on partners to take care of the video creation. This includes doing interviews with news stations or local neighborhood websites, especially when you're about to open for the first time or if you're hosting a special event.

If you have a founder, head chef, or other personality that gains popularity in the industry, then there's also the chance to engage in video partnerships with content channels such as Munchies or Bon Appetit, who employ dedicated videographers and editors. With those partnerships, you'll have access to professional audio, lighting, and even a stage kitchen for demonstration purposes. Videos on their YouTube channels garner hundreds of thousands of views, and are a boon to any business. However, these partnerships are hard to come by, unless it's part of your press junket, or your restaurant has a significant amount of buzz, or if you simply know the right connections.

PART II: MARKETING YOUR BUSINESS

6.
THE IMPORTANCE OF ONLINE MARKETING

The hardest part of marketing a new restaurant is starting from zero. More likely than not, you will have no brand recognition and you'll need to build equity piece by piece. First impressions matter, but so do the methods in which potential customers come across your business. Long gone are the days where you can rely solely on newspaper announcements and pedestrians passing by your newly opened restaurant. In order to keep up with the times, you'll have to adapt to modern internet marketing tactics like leveraging search engines, hosting events, maintaining email lists, and fostering partnerships.

This part of the book will cover the following marketing channels and tactics:

- Organic search & local SEO

- Pay-per-click (including paid search)

- Instagram

- Other social media

- Email newsletters

- Events

- Early adopters

- Marketing collateral

- Partnerships

7.
PAID VS. ORGANIC MARKETING

Generally speaking, marketing efforts can be divided into two buckets: paid and organic.

Paid marketing requires an ongoing budget, and typically, you pay based on its reach (how many people see your advertisements) or based on engagement (how many people click on them). Once you deplete or relinquish your budget, so too does your visibility dissipate. This includes (but is not limited to) tactics such as paid search, Facebook/Instagram ads, banners, and sponsored Yelp listings.

On the other hand, organic (or non-paid) marketing does not require ongoing budget and the benefits of these efforts can last indefinitely. This includes strategies like search engine optimization (SEO), publishing posts on social media platforms like Twitter/Facebook/Instagram, reviews you've received, and any mentions in publications that you did not pay for (all collectively referred to as "earned").

Which type of marketing do you need?

For best results, you'll want a mix of both types in order to craft the most comprehensive marketing strategy. You should consider organic tactics as your baseline level of marketing - *e.g.* make changes to your website so people can find you in Google; monitor what people say to/about you on Facebook and Yelp; build up your email userbase.

However, many of these strategies take time - which is when paid marketing is indispensable. As soon as you hit the right levers and buttons, your ads will go live and you'll immediately start getting eyeballs on your content. For instance, bid high enough on Google for the term "pizza in Midtown NYC," and you'll be somewhere near the top of their search results page within the ad space. Pay for sponsored listings on Yelp or Seamless, and again, you'll show up first when nearby people perform searches. Want to gain Instagram followers or get more likes for your "food porn" photos? Then pay for an ad campaign that targets the local foodie cohort.

The best way to think about it: your organic marketing strategy is how you want to be positioned in the long term, whereas your paid marketing strategy is how you can hit the ground running. Paid search can also help you acquire customers that you otherwise wouldn't be able to get in front of. Of course, with a properly integrated marketing strategy, you can use paid media to gain long term organic users (paying for ads that drive people to sign up for your mailing list, for example), but those are advanced tactics that require hands-on consultation.

Note that there is some grey area when you pay for an online service (such as MailChimp for email marketing). In these cases, the service is not amplifying your reach, so strictly speaking, it's not a paid media channel. The dollars go toward maintaining your database of users. For the sake of simplicity, I would classify email marketing as an organic tactic with monthly overhead. Likewise, paying for website hosting would not be a paid marketing strategy.

8.
ORGANIC SEARCH (SEO)

Organic search (aka natural search) should be a key marketing channel whenever you launch a website or create new content. Optimizing your site content ensures that search engines are able to find your pages, understand what they're about, and then serve them to users who search for something related.

All search engines have common goals - they want to catalog every single webpage on the internet (within reason), such that whenever a user performs a specific search, the engines can thumb through their "indexes" and return the best webpages that match what the user wants. Think of it like a library catalog system.

Understanding user intent is arguably the most important facet of a successful search engine experience. Whenever someone types something into the Google search bar, its algorithm determines what type of search it is, and what types of formats will best address the user's needs. For instance, if you search for a broad term like "curry powder," Google might return a combination of websites that sell spices or display online recipes, and possibly a Wikipedia article about the history of curry; this is because Google does not know exactly what you want and is providing options that will help narrow down your search. Conversely, if you type in a search phrase like "chicken tikka masala near me," Google will return some top 10 lists, or some aggregators like Yelp, and definitely a "local" map with the locations of multiple nearby restaurants.

To the user, this all happens in a split second. However, that's because Google has already done most of the legwork before you even conducted your search. In the previous example, think about all the things Google has to know:

- that chicken tikka masala is most commonly found at Indian restaurants

- that the user doesn't want how-to content, and probably doesn't want news items, images, or videos

- a rough idea of where the user is searching from (their mobile or GPS coordinates)

- a directory of all Indian restaurants within a reasonable radius of that location

- a list of menu items for those restaurants, so they can omit the businesses that don't serve chicken tikka masala

- the URLs of the pages on the remaining websites that will be most relevant for the user (for instance, a menu page, or a page featuring a photo of the dish)

All of these facets allow Google to populate its search engine results page (SERP) with the content they deem the most relevant (while also serving ads). Google may also alter its search results page if you're logged in based on what they know about you and your search history.

Search Engine Optimization (SEO)

Search engine optimization (also known as natural or organic search optimization) refers to actions that website owners can take in order to move their content higher up in the non-paid Google results. Engaging in "white hat" SEO practices are well within Google's guidelines, and are even encouraged. When your business reaches these top spots, "free" traffic will start to pour in, and new audiences will gain awareness of your business.

Any platform with a search bar can be considered a search engine, and content owners can optimize for most of them. Google Search is obviously a search engine, but so is Google Maps. And even YouTube (also owned by Google). Yelp is a search engine. And so is Seamless. Each one of these platforms has algorithms that determine what results appear on top, and business owners can, in theory, influence them.

However, for the sake of simplicity, let's focus just on Google Search (and by extension, Bing and Yahoo, etc.). Below are some general best practices for optimizing your content that all webmasters should implement:

• **Be clear and concise.** Each page should have a focus and ideally be about one overarching topic. For instance, your "Reservations" page shouldn't include information about the history of your restaurant. The main header (or headline) of your page should reflect what that page is about. If your page has multiple sections, then you should split them up with subheadings. In technical terms, the main header should be tagged as an <h1>. Most content management systems will do this automatically.

• **Optimize your page titles.** The page title is how you name your page within your content management system (CMS). This also serves as the text visible at the top of a user's browser window when they're on your website, and is also the blue underlined link that someone clicks on from the search engine results page. This is an opportunity to explain what your page is about, and to include your branding. For instance, a page title that says "Our Spring 2020 Dinner Menu | Maggie's Diner" is more descriptive than "Menu2.pdf." As a guideline, you should keep your page title under 65 characters (including spaces). Any more will be truncated in the SERP.

• **Add custom meta descriptions.** Within the SERP, the page title is followed by a small block of text. This is known as the meta description, and if you don't specify one, search engines will try to extract an excerpt from your page's content, which may not always make sense. Therefore, you should write your own. It should fall within 160 characters (including spaces), describe what your page is about without being redundant with the page title, and it should include a call to action (space permitting). Take advantage of the real estate you're allotted by Google.

• **Write content.** Search engines love text because it's the easiest format for them to understand. Search engines are getting more advanced, but they still cannot reliably interpret image and video content with a high degree of certainty. Therefore, all pages on your site should include at least one block of text (and ideally multiple). There's no strict guideline for how many words you should include, but it should be enough to provide proper context and to answer any questions a visitor might have.

• **Images and videos.** If your website content is image- or video-heavy, then you need to provide surrounding text to help search engines understand what's contained in those media files. For example, you should caption your pasta dish photo "Pappardelle with duck ragu" and name the image file pappardelle-with-duck-ragu-from-franks-restaurant.jpg. Videos too require some context. The video should not be the only content on a page. You should include a description of what the video is about, and if possible, a transcript.

• **Avoid duplicate content.** Understandably, Google believes it to be a bad user experience when multiple pages within a SERP say the same exact thing. So while it may be tempting to repurpose content from elsewhere, you should avoid this as it is easily detectable and search engines will penalize you. It's fine to quote short passages, but you should include a link to the original source as a standard practice.

Local SEO best practices

For the purposes of your business, you should focus specifically on local SEO; this refers to optimizing for any searches that Google categorizes as exhibiting local intent. This includes obvious examples, like searches including the term "near me" or ones that have zip code/location identifiers. But it can also be more abstract, like searches for a specific type of service (*e.g.* "French classes" or "oil change").

There are many facets to a successful local SEO strategy, but at the base level, the first thing you absolutely must do is ensure the accuracy of your business information. The three most important pieces of information are your business name, address, and phone number (so much so that they're colloquially abbreviated as "NAP"). Make sure your website includes all of the correct information, but also take a look at how other websites reference your business info - Google My Business, Yelp, Facebook, Bing Maps, and Apple Maps are the main platforms to audit.

There are many services that will, for a fee, ensure that all of your listings are accurate across multiple aggregators/online directories. However, for most small businesses, this is likely overkill. This will be covered in more detail in the next section.

Last, but certainly not least, content is your friend. Make sure you have photos of your business on all online directories where you're listed. User generated content (UGC) is also great - whether it's user reviews or photos. Both quality and quantity matter here.

Do you need a local SEO service?

You may have heard of local SEO vendors like Yext or Moz Local, and may have even been contacted by their salespeople. However, there's a good chance you don't need their services. Let's start with the basics of what these services do.

The key selling proposition of most local SEO vendors is that they scour the web to find any inconsistencies in your business listings (and correct inaccuracies on your behalf). However, as mentioned before, the lion's share of users will only use five directories - Google My Business, Yelp, Facebook, Bing Maps, and Apple Maps. Many of these local SEO services will include third tier websites (like Yellow Pages) as well as very niche directories that may not be relevant to your audience at all (like those for law offices or home maintenance). If you can manage your listings across the five main sites by yourself, then you should be in pretty good shape.

However, these services work wonders if you have multiple locations that constantly need updating. For instance, if you're a franchise or chain that routinely changes menu items, runs special deals, needs to update imagery for nationwide promotions, or has special holiday hours. In those cases, a local SEO vendor would probably be worth the cost.

There are two major instances where a small business might need one of these services - inaccurate listings and online reputation management.

If you find that your listings are inaccurate across multiple sites and you cannot correct them manually, then it may be prudent to consider a local SEO vendor. Many of these services have direct relationships with these listings sites and can make changes almost instantaneously (a luxury that regular users do not have). Do take the time to see if you can fix these problems yourself first, though.

Secondly, if you find that your online reviews are poor and you do not have the time (or skill, or patience) to address them, then local vendors can help repair your reputation. They have tools that make responding to feedback easier, and some services can even help you solicit new reviews. In all cases, it's a general best practice to learn how to listen and respond to your customers online. See Chapter 20 for more details on Online Reputation Management (ORM).

9.
PAY-PER-CLICK

Pay-per-click (PPC) refers to any advertising system where the advertiser pays each time a customer engages with the ad (typically by clicking on it). This includes platforms like Google AdWords, Facebook, and Instagram.

Running a PPC ad campaign

Starting a campaign on any of these platforms can be daunting, especially since you'll be spending real money. The best strategy will depend on your type of business and location, but here are some general best practices that apply to all platforms:

1. Set a budget cap.

This is by far the most important step. Depending on how your campaign is set up to target users, you could potentially burn through your entire budget in an hour. You should therefore set budget caps on a daily, monthly, or campaign level (*i.e.* for the life of your campaign until you manually renew your budget). But you should also set a per-bid cap. That way, if multiple businesses are bidding for the same customer, your price won't be driven up to a level that you would not feel comfortable paying. Without going into the technicalities, most PPC platforms will award the top ad placement to whoever agrees to pay the most, usually by increments of one cent. For instance, if you can only afford to pay 10 cents, and your competitor can pay 11, then their ad will be shown first (if their budget permits). In this scenario, placing a cap ensures that you will never pay more than 10 cents for a customer to view/engage with your ad.

2. Geo-target your audience.

There's no benefit of your ad appearing in front of someone in Wisconsin if your restaurant is in Boston. Alternatively, someone who searches for "Chicago style pizza" may actually be in Florida. It's best to let the platforms determine where the user is. To that end, you should set geo-targeting parameters on your campaigns and ads. Most advertising services allow you to do so at the state, city, or DMA/metro area level. This severely limits the number of unqualified users who will see your ads, and in theory, should reduce your overall costs.

You can even drill down to an even more granular level with geofencing. With geofencing, you drop a pin on a map, set a radius, and your ads will only be shown to people whose device location shows them within that area. This is known as hyperlocal advertising, and is an advanced technique.

3. Have a goal (or several).

What do you want users to do once they see your ads? Do you want them to book a reservation? Do you want them to place an online order? Or do you just want to generate awareness? It's important to establish these things early on, so you can retrospectively gauge the success of your campaign.

You can also set up multiple concurrent campaigns with different goals. For instance, set up one keyword/audience list for awareness, and another for reservation bookings.

Goals will also inform the type of creative you should publish, including the copy (the text in your ads) and imagery (if applicable).

4. Measure and assess.

Once your ad campaigns begin, you should start regularly monitoring their progress. If you're maxing out your daily budget and people stop seeing your ads by dinnertime, maybe you should increase your budget or decrease your frequency. If you're not getting the user volume you want, you may have to be more liberal with your targeting or expand your keyword lists.

5. A/B test.

After enough time has passed to achieve statistical significance, you should take a look at what worked and what didn't. Ad campaigns are not (and should not be) static. Use them as a learning experience to gain efficiencies in how you're spending your marketing dollars. If you find that a specific campaign is underperforming, you'll need to either pause it or make some improvements by adjusting one or more settings. A/B testing is the best way to achieve this, and most platforms have this functionality built in.

CPM campaigns

If you do not have a call to action as part of your ad, then you may consider buying on a CPM basis. CPM stands for cost-per-mille and is a set price for every 1,000 views of your ads (aka impressions). It will be harder to quantify user response, but these ads will help you increase awareness and visibility at a quick rate. This pricing structure is available on services like Facebook, Instagram, and Yelp, and you should follow the same set of aforementioned best practices.

The importance of research

As is the case with any kind of marketing, your outputs are only as good as your inputs. Performing your due diligence at the planning stage will ensure that your campaigns and testing methodologies are sound. This includes everything from audience research (are you targeting the right people?) to keyword research (are you bidding on terms that convert?). Doing this correctly requires hands-on consultation, and if you're serious about running ads, you should speak to a platform rep or hire an agency/professional.

There are many free keyword research tools on the market that can provide invaluable insight. The two most popular are Google's own AdWords Keyword Planner and Google Trends:

- **Google AdWords Keyword Planner**
(https://ads.google.com/home/tools/keyword-planner)
With this tool, you can type in specific phrases, and it will tell you how many times per month that term is searched. You can even edit the time frame to encompass several years into the past. This is useful as a rough gauge of how many people will see your ad based on your average bid, or how many people will see your page in the organic search engine results page if you maintain top positions. The higher the number, the greater the potential audience; however, these high volume terms are likely to be the most competitive.

- **Google Trends** (https://trends.google.com)
On the other hand, Google Trends is most useful for comparing different phrases or concepts over time (you can go as far back as 2004). If you're torn between two items or terms, Google Trends can tell you which is more popular (historically and currently), and will also make predictions about the future.

Both of these services allow you to segment audience data based on a specific location (city or state level). You should take advantage of this feature in order to add accuracy to your traffic projections and budgetary expectations.

10.
INSTAGRAM

Instagram is *the* social media platform du jour for foodies and aspiring influencers. Any respectable business should maintain some level of presence on Instagram. Having an account provides many benefits that can lead to increased business:

1. A captive audience.

With both posts and stories, Instagram allows content creators to take up the entire real estate of a user's screen. When someone's watching your story, that's all they're looking at. Take advantage of this by providing calls to action or creating instantly sharable content.

2. Discoverability.

Through the use of hashtags or the "Discover People" feature, more and more people will be able to find out that your business exists. Instagram hashtags also go a long way in helping market your posts. You should establish a set of hashtags to use on every post. Some common ones: the name of your restaurant, any tags specific to your city/state/region, and tags related to the food items, ingredients, or cuisine(s) featured. At the time of this writing, you're allotted up to 30 unique hashtags per post.

3. Location and account tagging.

Lastly, having an account allows others to tag you in their photos or to tag their photos with your location. This allows more people to more easily view your business information, and will enhance your online profile. As a business owner, this also lets you know what's resonating with users, and who you may want to reach out to for customer retention purposes. As an added bonus, you can use these posts as part of a curated photo carousel on your website.

Instagram is also the easiest way to go viral. Photo sharing is the new word of mouth. How many times has a particular dish gone viral due to its novelty or how ludicrous it is? There are businesses like Black Tap in Manhattan that create absurdly intricate and indulgent milkshakes that beg users to snap photos to share. There are "exclusive" or hard-to-get items like Dominique Ansel's cronut (and later inventions) that people will naturally brag about snagging. Plus, there's the entire genre of "food porn" where things that are normally not slathered in cheese sauce or deep fried... are. While they make give you a stomach ache later, they cause viewers to drool with jealousy/FOMO, and get them tapping the like/share buttons. Hopefully, these viewers will also convert into customers.

Aside from food, the interior and exterior design of a business is also a wonderful opportunity for people to snap photos. The best part? It's mostly passive and people don't even have to be customers to get involved. Consider things like street art on the facade of your business, cool wallpaper, unique neon signs, or otherwise amazing architecture. The more recognizable you can make your business, the better. One of the best examples of this is the bar Sisters in Clinton Hill, Brooklyn (@sistersbklyn on Instagram). Their giant chapel-shaped bar shelves and inviting skylight are instantly recognizable.

An important note about virality - it is <u>not</u> a marketing tactic. It is the outcome of a marketing strategy, albeit a rare one. You should weigh the costs and benefits or adding a new menu item or redecorating in the off-chance that it will draw customers in.

Lastly, regularly featuring behind-the-scenes content or the people who work at your restaurant/bar will help humanize your business. The employees you feature will also likely become your brand ambassadors on social media.

Facebook also has a stories capability that either duplicates or can be entirely separate from Instagram (since Facebook owns Instagram). The best practices don't vary wildly between the two, but for more information about how to best leverage the platform, check out storiescandoit.com (a site by Facebook for Business).

Buying followers and likes

Generally speaking, this is a poor investment. Instagram has a whole team dedicated to sussing out spammers and penalizing brands that engage in black hat tactics. However, if you absolutely cannot gain followers and have no choice but to pay for them, you should make sure:

- The accounts you're paying for are not all brand new and show regular activity.

- The accounts will engage with your content (liking or leaving comments).

- The accounts are near your location.

These things will be hard to find at a reasonable price, so it's best to avoid this strategy altogether.

Sponsored meals and contests

Another grey area is giving away meals or menu items in exchange for users posting about your business. Instagram has begun cracking down on this behavior, and it's now best practice for users to disclose the exchange using terms like "sponsored," "ad," or "complementary" on their posts. However, this does not mean you can't or shouldn't engage in sponsored meals (as long as you do it within the established guidelines).

Additionally, you can partner up with more established brands on Instagram for contests. This usually makes the most sense if you're hosting a ticketed event since those are the easiest prizes to give away. The expected rules to enter are typically easy to follow:

- users must like the post announcing the contest.

- users must follow both your account and the partner brand's account.

- additionally, the rules may also state that each person must tag X amount of friends in order to be entered (or that each tag counts as an incremental entry).

- for prizes of more substance or value, you may also ask users to share your post in their stories or as a separate Instagram post.

* * *

Spotlight on: Paulie Giannone

For a decade, Paulie Gee's has been one of the most revered pizza restaurants in all of New York. The man who started it all is Paulie Giannone, who can be regularly seen at his three NYC locations, personally greeting customers and managing the kitchen. Among his chief digital priorities is personally maintaining his social media accounts, most notably Instagram. I spoke to him about his approach to social marketing and how he infuses his persona into his posts:

On interacting with customers:
When I'm in a restaurant, I like being there and talking to people. I'm not doing it because I think it's good for the restaurant. Fortunately, I picked something that I enjoy doing that helps people. I like being out there, finding out what people are thinking.

On deciding what content to post:
Over [on the Paulie Gee's Slice Shop account], it's more specific to the pizza we serve and what goes on in the place. Over [on the main Paulie Gee's account], it's just me and restaurants. I don't get opinionated in terms of politics or religion. I like to mix my life with the business. And it's paid off well. I like the personal touch.

On finding customer feedback:
I check the [Instagram] location - top and recent every day. I'll do it for both locations. I also go to notifications to see if anyone tagged me.

People will come in and point to a post I made. It lets me know people find my stuff. I like a lot of comments. That's the one thing I love about Instagram - it's a very positive environment.

11.
OTHER SOCIAL MEDIA CONTENT

One of the most difficult aspects of maintaining an ongoing social media presence is finding something worthwhile to say. It'll be far too easy to discontinue posting regular updates altogether. However, doing so may have severe ramifications - for instance, customers may see an abandoned Instagram account and assume your business is no longer operational.

Here are some guidelines and content ideas that will help keep your online profiles current and accurate:

1. Business updates/announcements
This includes any new menu items, seasonal modifications, changes in hours, new policies, participation in local festivals, etc.

2. Weekly event reminders
If you host weekly events, then use this as an opportunity to remind your followers. You'd be surprised how forgetful people are when they're going about their lives, being inundated with irrelevant marketing messages all day.

3. Hashtags or themed days
If it makes sense for your brand, engage with well-established theme days (like Taco Tuesday or throwback Thursday). You'll get more exposure for utilizing popular hashtags, and it'll be a fun excuse to be cheeky and post content that may not necessarily be new or original.

4. Content from others

You can also repost photos that others have shared featuring your business. If you're using it for marketing purposes, you should obtain permission first. However, on platforms like Instagram or Facebook, if your business is tagged, most of the time you can simply repost with a proper attribution to their account. See the Photography section in Chapter 5 for more information.

5. Customer reviews

Featuring content from others isn't limited to photos. You can also include quotes from customer reviews in order to highlight recent or extraordinary experiences. This lends credibility to the quality of your product and service.

6. Business mentions

Speaking of credibility, if your business is mentioned in a news/magazine article, then it behooves you to share that with your audience. It will encourage discussion and sharing on their part. This is especially important if you've been nominated for an award, received some sort of status (*e.g.* Michelin Bib Gourmand), or have been featured on a food writer's top 10 list somewhere. The authors and publishers will also be incentivized to share your reactions.

7. Polls

Polls are a quick, low effort way for your customers to engage with your content and share their thoughts. For the most part, you should be polling about items relevant to your business (*e.g.* What's your favorite appetizer of ours? Should we bring back our bacon Old Fashioned? Do you want us to show the baseball or college basketball game on our projector tonight?). But sometimes, cultural events are so significant that you can have some fun and post about them as well (*e.g.* Did you enjoy that Game of Thrones series finale? Who do you want to win the Super Bowl?).

* * *

In order to manage all of these tactics, a content calendar will be your best tool. It will remind you of what needs to be posted and when. And if you need to create new content (*e.g.* photos or writing), it should provide you ample time to gather the proper assets.

Lastly, it's important that all of your social media messaging is on-brand. If you have multiple people posting, then you should ensure there's a consistent tone and vocabulary. If there are multiple people responding to customers (publicly or in private), then you should have message sign-offs so people know who they're talking to.

12.
EMAIL NEWSLETTERS

While automated email newsletters have a bad reputation of being ignored, ones for restaurants are different. For starters, it's almost impossible for someone to accidentally opt into one. Additionally, local businesses have an inherent human connection, and email recipients are almost guaranteed to be planning a future meal.

That said, it's still important to avoid flooding your customer base with too many emails. Nobody wants to receive weekly messages along the lines of "swing by this Friday because we're having our regular menu and no drink specials!" The best newsletters contain new information, ideally of the time sensitive sort.

The best information is the kind that benefits the customer. Customers respond well to deals or specials, for instance. If you've never had a happy hour before and are just starting one, that's worthy of an email. If you're participating in a local event like a Restaurant Week or a food festival, people will be interested in that as well. If you're known for your seasonal menus, users will probably want to know when that changeover happens. Holiday emails are also acceptable, especially if you're communicating special hours, or explaining that you're still taking reservations for Valentine's Day or Christmas dinner, for instance.

Websites are the best way to collect email addresses. Including a module on your homepage, or within your navigation is a proven method of doing so. Make sure, however, that you don't use people's email addresses for other purposes. If someone signed up to hear more from your business, they will not want to hear about unrelated enterprises (this may even cause you to be filed under spam filters, which are hard to escape). The one exception is if you're part of a group of restaurants; then, it's permissible to tell users that a new sister location is opening (especially if there's some sort of opening day/week special). See the Hosting Events section in Chapter 13 for more information.

Lastly, I would not recommend handling all of your own end-to-end email communications. There are numerous services that can make the process easier. This ranges from helping compose/design the body of the emails to providing robust analytics tracking (which will make it easier to know what types of links or calls to action resonate the most).

With the proper filters, you can also track what email newsletter subscribers do once they reach your website. These automated services also make unsubscribing easier and less prone to error. On that note, your newsletters should always have an option to unsubscribe! Always!

* * *

Spotlight on: Daniel Delaney

I spoke with Dan Delaney about his widely popular pop-up concept BrisketLab, which was many New Yorkers' introduction to his barbecue. It eventually led to a brick and mortar barbecue location, as well as other restaurant locations around New York. For BrisketLab and beyond, his business relied heavily on email marketing. Here is some of his advice:

On email marketing:
"Email is the best form of marketing. You can have a captive, focused audience willing to engage with whatever you're selling. That's better than any ad you're placing on Facebook or Instagram."

On crafting the best voice for email:

"Email was a way to create intimacy with the brand. They were written by me in a casual, first-person narrative. You may be hard-pressed to find another restaurant in New York that had patrons that felt as connected to a restaurant as those going to BrisketLab and BrisketTown. It felt like being part of a club."

13.
HOSTING EVENTS

Events are a great way to gain exposure for your business, and they allow you to collect feedback while also generating photos/reviews. For new restaurants, a soft opening party for selected guests will provide a head start on marketing efforts. However, figuring out who makes the cut for the guest list requires a targeted strategy. Depending on how big the opening is, you can invite local magazine and newspaper reviewers. And if you're a new addition to the neighborhood, it doesn't hurt to loop in folks from the business improvement district (it's in their best interest for the neighborhood to thrive, after all).

Past that, you'll want to identify social media influencers, which can be a laborious task. The easiest (and least successful) method would be to "cold" message anybody in the area with a large number of followers. However, with a few parameters, you can ensure higher success rates. On Instagram, you should look for accounts with high engagement - this includes follower counts, likes, and comments. Since it's easy to buy followers (see Chapter 10), the latter two metrics are far more important. Make sure the account has a captive audience that engages with the posted content. Additionally, you can perform location searches for similar businesses in the area, and once you're there, look at the most popular posts. Chances are if someone has an affinity for a similar or nearby restaurant, they'll be open to giving yours a shot as well.

On a platform like Yelp, a relevant reviewer will be someone who writes great content and gives favorable reviews. Again, you can check to see who's visited similar businesses in the area and target those users. Yelp allows you to directly message users as long as you have an account. In order to host a more formal Yelp event, you have some options that will be covered in the following section.

In any case, it's important to note that you will be operating at a loss for such events. There may also be unexpected conditions that depress turnout, like inclement weather or traffic jams. Or you may invite too many people and run up costs (or worse, run out of food and drinks). So plan accordingly!

An alternative is to host a (heavily discounted) soft open week, which works well and mitigates some risk. Inviting guests to dine at your restaurant before the official open has many benefits: you provide patrons with more opportunities to schedule a visit; you can capture email addresses and other contact information for future communications; the extra time allows word of mouth to spread (especially if the first visitors are pleased with their experiences); and lastly, if you host this soft open well in advance, you'll have proper lead time to collect feedback and make adjustments before opening to the public. Just be sure that all of your service licenses are up to date and valid.

For friends and family events, Facebook is definitely the best platform for inviting folks. Unless you need check-in capabilities at the door, a service like Eventbrite is probably not worth the hassle. Plus, most people have and regularly check Facebook, and will likely spread the word about your event (deliberately, or as a result of their public RSVP showing up in friends' news feeds).

Hosting a Yelp Event

Organizing events is a job unto itself. Hosting an event via Yelp is a great way to leverage the expertise of seasoned event coordinators, gain the attention of an established audience, and take a lot of the guesswork out of the equation.

There are two types of events: Unofficial Yelp Events, and Official Yelp Events. An Unofficial Yelp Event (UYE) simply consists of creating a public calendar listing open to the entire Yelp community. There, you can provide the details of when, where, and what you're hosting. It allows you to easily gauge the responsiveness of the audience and reach out to users who have responded. Past that, the rest of the legwork is up to you.

An Official Yelp Event (OYE), on the other hand, provides you with the support of your local Community Manager. They will act as an event planner - this means they'll cull guest lists and can even help coordinate a liquor/alcohol vendor to partner with you, reducing overhead. Yelp events are typically hosted by emerging businesses looking to increase awareness, or by struggling businesses looking to drum up additional business/word of mouth.

Note that there are a few important points that you should keep in mind before agreeing to host an OYE:

- Typically, the Community Manager will create a discrete Yelp listing for the event that's separate from your main business page. This will allow users to be honest without having their experience of your business colored by the free night out. Giving away anything in exchange for a review is against Yelp guidelines, so this is their compromise.

- Yelpers can be harsh critics. Many of them expect quick service, and to leave with full stomachs and in an inebriated state. In my experience, the most scathing reviews for events usually stem from poor planning (where food and drink are depleted early on, or if the space is overcrowded). Avoid these scenarios at all costs!

- People who attend these events are under no obligation to return as paying customers. However, if you make it an enjoyable experience and make a genuine effort to meet the Yelpers, they'll likely return with friends or spread the word. Capturing their contact information or giving them a discount on a future visit helps as well.

• Leave a tip jar out! People receiving free food and drinks are usually more generous and appreciative of the staff.

Hosting other meetups or events

If you have a generously sized space, you can also use your location to host meetups. I've attended events at bars/restaurants for all purposes: industry keynotes, board game nights, weekly trivia, comedy shows, science talks, karaoke nights, etc. The key is to have these events regularly at predictable intervals to gain repeat customers. This is also a great way to supplement what would otherwise be off-nights. Just make sure you have the technology and capacity to host these types of events.

14.

INCENTIVIZING EARLY ADOPTERS

FOMO (or the "fear of missing out") is one of the most influential forces in social media. Does everybody on your Instagram feed seem to be going to the same bakery for a special, limited edition cupcake? Maybe you should go too before they're sold out! A lot of respected food writers seem to be checking in at a new neighborhood restaurant. Maybe you should go before the New York Times reviews it, and it becomes impossible to reserve a table!

While it's tough to predict which businesses or specific menu items will take off, there are a few best practices to encourage success:

1. Create buzz

This means establishing your presence early and often. For new menu items, this could mean posting Instagram/Facebook posts leading up to the release date. As the day nears, you should start posting more photos that users can share with their friends. The audience response can also help you set expectations on in-person demand.

2. Get influencers involved

Inviting influencers (such as food journalists or those who run social media accounts) to try out your latest and greatest products will kickstart word of mouth. Additionally, you can also receive invaluable critical feedback that will benefit the larger public.

3. Hand out physical gifts

Creating limited edition gifts, like t-shirts, phone cases, or tote bags, will increase the level of exclusivity of your opening or special event, and doubles as advertising for your business.

4. Leverage email lists

Use your email newsletters to keep your client base up to date on the latest goings-on at your business.

5. Offer check-in benefits

Through apps with a check-in feature (such as Yelp or Foursquare/Swarm/Facebook), you can offer benefits like a free side/drink or a percentage discount off of the bill. You can also limit this to the first time someone checks in. I've also been to restaurants that provide perks to patrons if they post an Instagram post or story about the business.

15.
MARKETING
COLLATERAL

Now for the fun stuff. Once you've established your branding, you should design some marketing collateral. This includes simple things like business cards, and the postcards that come paper-clipped to the bill. But also more fun things like pens (that people will most definitely steal) and matchbooks. On all of these items, you should be sure to include your website address, and contact information (address and phone number) if space permits.

One of the more unique freebies I've recently received was a branded guitar pick from the restaurant Frenchette in Tribeca, Manhattan. While I don't think every restaurant needs to go this level of effort, the attention to detail doesn't go unnoticed.

Some more standard options include pins and stickers (which younger people love for some reason).

16.
PARTNERSHIPS

Sometimes, it makes sense for your business to partner with other businesses. For instance, you might start exclusively serving coffee from a local roaster with a loyal following; you could feature alcohol from a startup distillery that has a unique story; or you could collaborate on a new menu item in conjunction with another restaurant (and even host a limited edition popup with them). Whenever you do such activities, you're able to leverage the established audiences of both parties for mutual benefit.

One increasingly common business arrangement is to have restaurants or food trucks spend a day selling food at a business without a kitchen (like a bar or brewery). There are also companies (such as Fooda) that bring a similar service to office buildings.

Deals sites

Websites like Groupon, LivingSocial, and Pulsd can also increase in-person business (at a cost, of course). Partnering with these sites means reaching an audience who might have otherwise never known you existed. However, determining whether or not to partner with these services requires some number crunching. It's also worth noting that for many struggling restaurants, these deal sites are a last resort for revenue. One of the more common uses of these sites is to sell tickets to events (especially if sales are lagging).

PART III: KEEP CUSTOMERS COMING BACK

17.
CUSTOMER RETENTION

Repeat business is often what separates success from failure. Brand loyalty is hard to come by, especially when people are presented with countless options on a daily basis. But it's worth its weight in salt, as the familiar is a welcome solution to people's choice paralysis. And happy customers will likely recommend your business to their friends and family.

But how can you encourage customers to return time and again? The obvious first step is to ensure they have a pleasant initial experience. Past that, ongoing communication through various mediums is key. You'd be surprised how forgetful people are of positive experiences they've had.

18.
LOYALTY PROGRAMS

The physical sandwich punch card is quickly becoming a relic of the past. Like most everything else, it's been modernized with digital solutions. Rewarding customers for their patronage is now significantly easier since they can simply tap their phones, or order through apps and have every transaction automatically recorded.

Many services like LevelUp and Belly allow customers to check in to a business and receive relevant deals in real time. No more carrying cards in your wallet and risking losing them!

Of course, you should make sure your rewards are worth the effort. Punch cards took up physical real estate in people's wallets and required intent and dedication to fill up. It also required planning on the businesses' part and an understanding of typical customer behaviors (namely in-store frequency). As such, cards typically had a larger reward attached to their completion (like a free sandwich or an appetizer).

But now, digitization has made it incredibly easy to fine-tune the reward distribution model and allow businesses to test out different incentives. Customers and businesses alike can operate in a lower commitment environment, with smaller perks at higher frequencies - think items like free salad toppings or a size upgrade on a coffee. Apps also make it easy to create multiple concurrent incentive programs and to change specific rewards if they are underperforming.

19.
GIFT CARDS

Purchasing gift cards is the ultimate sign of loyalty. Customers are not only recommending you to their friends; they're also guaranteeing that you'll be seeing future in-person business. The notion of offering gift cards may seem daunting at first, but many services can help out (such as CustCon and Toast).

However, it's worth noting that gift cards may not be right for every business. They're typically best in these three scenarios:

- **Fast/fast casual**
Gift cards will be purchased/used more often if they make the recipient's life more convenient. They're best for regular purchases at coffee chains or made-to-order salad franchises near the home/workplace. They make reliable (last-minute) office gifts as well, especially for new employees.

- **Hospitality groups**
People may be hesitant to purchase gift cards that are only valid at one physical location. However, if you're part of a restaurant group, then you can (and should) allow your gift cards to be used at various locations. This provides the gift recipient more choices, and will pique their interest in other restaurant options; they will likely hop online to research the different locations before making a reservation.

- **Other merchandise**
If your business extends beyond food and drink (*i.e.* you sell other physical goods), then the recipient has an even

wider selection to choose from. Receiving a gift card is instead transformed into a shopping experience. If you sell branded merchandise (like t-shirts, totes, caps, etc.), prepackaged goods (like your house recipe sauce), glassware, or if you pull double duty as a neighborhood grocer with a selection of shelf-stable products, then gift cards are a no-brainer.

You should also allow people to purchase gift cards online, with the ability to check their existing/leftover balances. Again, this will likely require engaging with an external vendor, but you should do things right if you're doing them at all.

20.
ONLINE REPUTATION MANAGEMENT (ORM)

Your branding is how people perceive or recall your business. With brands posting on social media as if they're people, businesses are increasingly humanizing themselves. As such, you should take advantage of the opportunities to monitor and respond to feedback, which is now expected behavior.

On platforms like Yelp or Google, regularly monitor for new reviews and respond (good and bad). If the reviews mention information/viewpoints you have not considered, then you can also make changes accordingly. If a review is exceedingly negative or inaccurate, you should publicly clear the air (without being combative). Offer to make things right if the reviewer seems open to returning - this doesn't have to be as heavy-handed as a free meal, but a personal invitation or a free appetizer/dessert can go a long way; just be sure to handle the specific details privately. People are surprisingly understanding once they experience a personal connection.

Local listings vendors and dedicated reputation monitoring services can help you stay abreast of new content related to your business. They can also help you set up a system where customers will receive emails or text messages after they visit your location to encourage them to leave feedback (see chapter 8 for more information on local SEO vendors).

At the very least, you should set up Google alerts to automatically receive new mentions of your business. You should also turn on your notifications across social media networks for any mentions of your business name or profile handle. This will provide you with an ongoing temperature of customer perceptions over time.

21.
MAILING LISTS

It bears repeating that email newsletters are a time-tested method of driving foot traffic. See the Email Newsletters section in Chapter 12 for more information.

PART IV:
IF THINGS TURN
SOUR…

22.
START ANEW
OR SALVAGE?

The sad reality is that not all business can thrive. This can be the result of miscalculating business opportunities, overwhelming negative press, or other hardships. But if you're not ready to give up yet, there are two major paths you can take: either try to salvage your existing brand/web presence, or start again from scratch with what you've learned.

At the end of the day, you'll have to make this tough business decision, but the following sections will include some guidelines and considerations for whichever path you take.

23.
REBRANDING

If you've found that not enough locals are interested in your type of cuisine and you want to pivot, you should make sure it's apparent what's changed. For example, if you change from Himalayan food to general Asian fusion, then you should explicitly add the latter to your business name on all online platforms to drive home the change (renaming will also allow you to appear as a "new" business on some online services). There will be the added benefit of being visible for the new terms you've added.

On a personal note, I've returned to restaurants where their entire concept has flipped, and they did not adequately advertise these drastic change. Expecting a fast casual meal when the business is now a sit-down restaurant (and vice versa) can be jarring. Going out of your way for a specific menu item and finding out that the restaurant stopped serving it months ago without notice is also a big letdown. Do all you can to avoid these scenarios!

Social media will be very helpful in pushing out the message that you've made some changes/improvements. See chapters 10 and 11 for social media best practices.

24.
RENAMING

What if you need to rename your business entirely? Chinese restaurants in New York City do this all the time (often, it's directly following a bad health inspection score, or simply so they qualify for "new business" tax credits). We can learn a few things from these restaurants - even with constant name changes, they maintain a steady customer base. Chinese communities exhibit impeccable word of mouth communication, and in a lot of these cases, they're only changing their English name while maintaining their Chinese name, which has more brand recognition.

If you're not in this very specific situation, then you'll have to deliberate carefully about whether or not to change your name. One of the biggest reasons to do so would be if you've received an insurmountable amount of negative press/feedback. However, note that changing your name will have many complications:

- **Brand recognition**
Any brand equity that you've built up for the previous business will essentially be erased, and you'll essentially be starting from zero (unless you have an established community following already, like in the aforementioned Chinese restaurant example).

- **Updating listings**
Updating your business information on Google My Business, Yelp, etc. may become an incredibly involved ordeal, and there's no guarantee that any changes will stick

if the platforms can't validate them. If you want to divorce yourself from the previous business name, you'll need to mark the old business as "closed" and then create a new business listing. However, at times, these services may combine the old and new listings, and you'll inherit all the negative reviews or now-inaccurate information; this is the worst case scenario. If this happens, then you may have to shell out for a local listings vendor to help correct this, which will be an added monthly cost (see chapter 8).

• **Website management**

In addition to creating a new website, it is to your benefit to keep your old website. You can either add messaging that informs visitors that you've closed and link users to your new site, or you can just redirect people immediately such that they never encounter the old content (this would require a technical configuration, but the benefit is that any organic search value and rankings of the old site would be passed to the new one). Note that maintaining the old website will have associated annual domain and hosting costs associated with it, however.

25.
FURTHER READING

I hope that this book has given you a good idea of all the inputs that go into a successful local business marketing campaign. My goal with this information was twofold:

- I want to empower you to improve your online presence and recognize that there are many things that you can start doing today.
- I want to be fully transparent that some pivotal marketing tactics are incredibly involved (and not exactly "easy"), and you may need a bespoke strategy from an expert or agency to kickstart things.

Additionally, you can (and should) use this book as a checklist for any of your marketing activities, even if you're engaging with a third party service. This will help keep everyone honest, and will let you prioritize the direction of your efforts.

If you want to arm yourself with more knowledge about the intricacies of online marketing, there are many resources I can recommend; I will maintain an updated list of preferred vendors and references at restsite.com/marketing-resources

Another great starting point is the Google Digital Garage curriculum. It is a free set of online courses from Google that focus on everything from starting an online business to using their advertising platforms. The "Fundamentals of Digital Marketing" course has many different chapters covering the basics, and I highly recommend that you give it a look. The URL to access this content is learndigitalwithgoogle.com/digitalgarage

PART V: INTERVIEWS WITH THE EXPERTS

This final section includes full transcripts of interviews that I've conducted with business owners and other experts who have been kind enough to share their time and expertise with me.

I will continue to add more interviews to my website at restsite.kennychung.net/restaurant-owner-interviews

PAULIE GIANNONE

Paulie Gee's and Paulie Gee's Slice Shop

Paulie Giannone is one of the most recognizable pizzaiolos in New York City. Step into his original restaurant, Paulie Gee's, and you'll be greeted with a handshake (and if you're lucky, a pin). You'll recognize him from his thick rimmed glasses and trucker hats that advertise his favorite pizzerias from all over the country. I spoke with Paulie at his Slice Shop in Greenpoint, Brooklyn in September 2019. We discussed his usage of social media and how the landscape of restaurant marketing has changed in the 9 years since he opened his first pizza restaurant.

In the pizza world, you're a well-known personality. I've been to your original location many times, and you're always walking around shaking hands and talking to people. How do you translate in-person personality to online?

When I'm in a restaurant, I like being there and talking to people. I'm not doing it because I think it's good for the restaurant. Fortunately, I picked something that I enjoy doing that helps people. I know people in the restaurant business and they don't necessarily like talking to people - they gotta go hide in the kitchen. I like being out there, finding out what people are thinking. I have a curiosity about people. So people see that.

Over here [on the Paulie Gee's Slice Shop account], it's more specific to the pizza we serve and what goes on in the place. Over there [on the main Paulie Gee's account], it's just me and restaurants. I don't get opinionated in terms of politics or religion. I may get opinioned on people being really stupid once in a while.

I like to mix my life with the business. And it's paid off well. My guy in Chicago, Derek in Logan Square, he does the same thing. My guy at Paulie Gee's Columbus, TJ, all he posts is pizza. I like the personal touch.

Are you getting a lot of in-person feedback to posts you've made on social media?

Oh yeah, people will come in and point to a post I made. It lets me know people find my stuff. I like a lot of comments. That's the one thing I love about Instagram - it's a very positive environment. You don't get a lot of people ragging on you.

How do you find photos of your business?

I don't do hashtags. I check the location - top and recent every day. I'll do it for both locations. I also go to notifications to see if anyone tagged me.

You had reached out to me on Instagram about a photo I had posted, wanting a full-size version. What was the motivation behind that?

Magazines reach out and want photos. Just today I got something from USA Today. They wanted a picture of my pizza. I get that a lot. I have a lot of photos, but most of it's on my phone. So I just decided that I needed to get more high resolution stuff.

For online listings - like Yelp, Facebook Place pages - do you have someone who maintains those listings for accuracy?

Yes. I do it. For the Slice Shop, Andrew does it too. Otherwise, I pretty much do it, which can be very frustrating. Especially when other sites post your menus. I don't want them there, because then I have to worry about them.

How do you handle responding to negative comments?

That's the one that frustrates me is Facebook and Pages - people leave comments and reviews, and I don't even know. Facebook is confusing. There are notifications for your personal account, and notifications for the business all in the same place.

Google is frustrating too. I get a notification every time someone leaves a review on Yelp, but I don't get anything on Google. We have another email address and someone has to forward it to me. I don't like somebody saying something that may require a response because I don't like to respond. The only time I respond is something on Yelp or Google reviews is if I need to apologize for something. Otherwise, I don't like to give the impression that I'm working the crowd. So I stick to Instagram.

Are there any difficulties with primarily marketing through Instagram?

The hard thing is you can't post a link. I won't do the "link in bio" thing. I refuse to do that because eventually there will be something else in that link. I don't do stories. It's very frustrating. You go to look for it, and the next day it's gone.

Do you ever take days off from social media?

No! Ask my wife.

You never know what's gonna pop up.

Last question - what advice would you give to someone starting out in the business?

Yeah, just do it. If it's something you love, take the risk or nothing's gonna happen. That's my best advice.

DANIEL DELANEY

BrisketTown, BrisketLab, Delaney Chicken

Dan Delaney burst onto the NYC food scene with his pop-up concept BrisketLab, where he pre-sold meat by the half pound and set up events at bars and office spaces. Since then, he moved onto permanent spaces including his barbecue restaurant BrisketTown in Brooklyn, and several Delaney Chicken restaurants, serving fried chicken sandwiches. I spoke with him over the phone in September 2019, as he was in Mexico City planning a new burger restaurant concept. We discussed how BrisketLab came to fruition, and the importance of creating pre-launch buzz and email marketing in general.

BrisketLab was such a unique concept. How did you come up with it?

Before I brought up my smoker from Texas, I was talking to a lot of friends in the barbecue restaurant space. They told me there would be a lot of potential problems with doing it the way I originally wanted to, especially in the eyes of the health department. I didn't have the money or infrastructure to build a real kitchen. BrisketLab had a more elusive feel largely as a result of practical reasons - from me not wanting to get in trouble with the law. But the result was that it also created buzz and extra excitement.

Heading into the summer of 2012, I remember reading about BrisketTown on Twitter and in food blogs. How did you originally seed the idea and get the word out?

Before starting on this endeavor, I had already been making video content for the internet and writing an email newsletter [called Eater's Digest], so I was quasi-connected. I also studied and have a degree in technology, so it was pretty much in my wheelhouse.

Did you reach out to journalists specifically?

I had emailed most mainstream publications like the [New York] Times and Eater, and I said "we're about to do the most exciting food event of the summer in New York City. If you don't write about it, your audience will be frustrated that they didn't hear about it." And it worked, and they wrote about it.

How did the website play into your marketing?

I wasn't sure how I would do fundraising, but I wanted to get a read on the response from potential constituents. So what I did was launch a "coming soon" website to collect email addresses. We collected over 7,000 email addresses over a week. We realized that if we just dumped those people into Kickstarter, they would feel disappointed because they thought they were signing up for something more exclusive. I was also worried that people wouldn't be looking to buy a lot of meet, and that there needed to be urgency.

How did you foster immediacy?

We built a proprietary web interface that let us query our inventory of meat to display on our homepage. When people made a purchase, the quantity of remaining meat went down. We also built a calculator because we feared people would just buy one pound and that wouldn't be enough funding for us. We let people specify how many events they wanted to go with and the number of friends they would bring. It would then suggest an amount of meat; the average order was three pounds of meat, or $75 worth.

And did you also leverage your email list?

To keep up the idea of FOMO [fear of missing out], I started to send out emails 500 at a time. It would tell people "you're the first 500 people and we're giving you access to the website for an hour, and then we'll invite the next 500 people."

Once BrisketLab was over, did you use your email lists to gauge interest in a brick-and-mortar location?

The truth was I didn't start BrisketLab with the goal of starting BrisketTown or to become a business owner. I did BrisketTown because I had all these people saying BrisketLab was the best barbecue they've ever had and that I should keep doing it. "Here's a check, why don't you open a restaurant?"

How did your marketing efforts change once you opened a physical restaurant?

Very differently. It was a combination of right place, right time. We opened up when New York City was starting to become hungry for barbecue. I was gladly accepting tons of press; if someone wanted to write something, I would always do interviews. The unusual way we got our funding made for a good story.

Why did you continue with email marketing instead of other channels?

I've always felt when people say they spend nothing on marketing, that's a stupid attitude. Marketing is a smart thing, not a bad thing. In general, email is the best form of marketing. You can have a captive, focused audience willing to engage with whatever you're selling. That's better than any ad you're placing on Facebook or Instagram.

I remember your emails had a unique and personal tone. Was that done intentionally?

Email was a way to create intimacy with the brand. They were written by me in a casual, first-person narrative. You may be hard-pressed to find another restaurant in New York that had patrons that felt as connected to a restaurant as those going to BrisketLab and BrisketTown. It felt like being part of a club.

What advice would you give to your younger self?

I transitioned to brick-and-mortar knowing literally nothing about running a restaurant or about business. If I had the opportunity to do it again, I wish I would have somebody to help me navigate the waters more. There was never a business plan. I didn't understand how much to charge. I built it totally wrong.

How did those experiences inform your next project?

We're about to open up a new restaurant in Mexico City, but I'm doing it with a restaurant group, not as a solo act. We have a team of people running the restaurant, so that's not my job anymore. It's quite different!

ABOUT THE AUTHOR

I am a native New Yorker with a background in mass communication and advertising. I have worked in digital marketing for over a decade, consulting top brands and small businesses on how to improve their online presence. Among the brands I have consulted on for local digital strategy: Verizon Wireless, Jaguar/Land Rover, Pitney Bowes, and Belle Tire. Additionally, I worked with American Express on their Small Business Saturday campaign.

I have always been an adamant supporter of local businesses, and have the numbers to show it. To date, have written over 3,500 Yelp reviews (with an additional 14,000+ photos/videos uploaded). I have been quoted in Eater, Food & Wine, AdWeek, and Buzzfeed. My business photos have been featured in Time Out Magazine, ABC News, The Weather Channel, MSN, Yahoo News, and the Daily Mail.

I have made many resources available for free at restsite.com, and can be reached via email at hello@restsite.com. I am also available on Instagram and Twitter at @kennySHARKchung.

www.ingramcontent.com/pod-product-compliance
Lightning Source LLC
Chambersburg PA
CBHW030951240526
45463CB00016B/2335